# Understanding Assurance & Salvation

*Robert E. Picirilli*

Randall House Publications
114 Bush Road
PO Box 17306
Nashville, TN 37217

800-877-7030
www.RandallHouse.com

**Understanding Assurance & Salvation**
Robert E. Picirilli

Published by Randall House Publications
114 Bush Road
Nashville, Tennessee 37217

© Copyright 2006
Randall House Publications

Printed in the United States of America
ISBN 0892656360
Library of Congress Control Number: 2006928657

# Table of Contents

# Preface

Calvinism is the name of the theology of salvation traced to John Calvin (1509-64), the leading theologian of the early Protestant Reformation, a magisterial reformer of almost as much importance as Martin Luther himself. Arminianism represents the thinking of Jacobus Arminius (1560-1609), a Dutch thinker who resisted some of the forms of Calvinism.

Since the Calvinistic-dominated Synod of Dort in 1618-19, it has become customary to summarize the differences between the two schools of thought using the acrostic TULIP.

**T** is for *Total Depravity*. Calvin insisted that humans are so depraved, following original sin, that they are permanently disabled from responding to God until He first regenerates them. Arminius did not disagree about the depravity, but he understood the Bible to teach that God's pre-regenerating grace enables the depraved person—still possessing freedom of the will as part of his constitutional makeup—to respond positively or negatively to the offer of salvation in Christ.

**U** is for *Unconditional Election*. Calvin believed that God by predestination chose some to be saved and the rest to be lost, eternally, and unconditionally. Arminius agreed that it is biblical to speak of the election as eternal, but he held that it is likewise biblical to speak of election as based on the saving faith of the individuals, exercised in time.

**L** is for *Limited Atonement*. Calvin taught that Christ died only for those whom God had unconditionally elected. Arminius cited a wealth of biblical evidence that Christ died for the entire human race and thus provided salvation for all—applied, however, only to those who respond in faith to the gospel.

**I** is for *Irresistible Grace*. Calvin's view was that elected persons are regenerated by the gracious work of the Holy Spirit without their awareness or cooperation; only after this new birth can they receive faith as a gift from God. Arminius understood the Bible to teach, instead, that the individual, enabled by the Spirit but not yet regenerated, must willingly believe in Christ in order to be saved.

**P** is for *Perseverance*. Calvin said that all who are elected will necessarily persevere in salvation. Arminius, though he did not develop this doctrine as fully as the others, referred to biblical teachings that ought to make one cautious, passages that fall short of guaranteeing that all who are born again will certainly persevere to the end.

This little book treats the views of Arminius, and of more recent followers of his thinking—including this writer—on this fifth subject.

# Chapter One

# Arminianism and Conditional Perseverance

As I have said in the preface, Arminius himself and his first followers[1] avoided a clear conclusion on the subject of perseverance. But they raised the question, and the natural implications of their non-predestinarian view of salvation, even at that early stage, tended to question whether Calvinism's assumption of necessary perseverance was truly biblical.

Arminius' opinion on the subject can be captured in this relatively brief statement on the subject:

> My sentiments respecting the perseverance of the Saints are, that those persons who have been grafted into Christ by true faith, and have thus been made partakers of his life-giv-

---

[1] They were called "Remonstrants" because (in 1610) they presented a remonstrance, outlining their views, to the States of Holland.

ing Spirit, possess sufficient powers [or strength] to . . . gain the victory over those enemies—yet not without the assistance of the grace of the same Holy Spirit. . . . So that it is not possible for them, by any of the cunning craftiness or power of Satan, to be either seduced or dragged out of the hands of Christ. But I think it is useful and will be quite necessary in our first convention, to institute a diligent enquiry from the Scriptures, whether it is not possible for some individuals through negligence to desert the commencement of their existence in Christ, to cleave again to the present evil world, to decline from the sound doctrine which was once delivered to them, to lose a good conscience, and to cause Divine grace to be ineffectual.

Though I here openly and ingenuously affirm, I never taught that *a true believer can either totally or finally fall away from the faith, and perish;* yet I will not conceal, that there are passages of Scripture which seem to me to wear this aspect; and those answers to them which I have been permitted to see, are not of such a kind as to approve themselves on all points to my understanding.[2]

From a historical perspective, Arminius insisted that the denial of such a possibility "was never, from the very times of the apostles down to the present day, accounted by the church as a catholic doctrine," and that the view that holds apostasy to be possible "has always

---

[2] James Arminius, *The Writings of James Arminius* (three vols.), tr. James Nichols and W. R. Bagnall (Grand Rapids: Baker, 1956), I:254.

had more supporters in the church."[3] And in his long "examination" of the treatise on predestination by William Perkins, he undertook to show that Perkins' arguments against the possibility of apostasy were not sufficient to make the case certain—even after he entered the discussion by remarking,"That true and saving faith may be, totally and finally, lost, I should not at once dare to say."[4]

The very fact that he and his followers raised this question, however, indicates that this view was sure to follow from the basic principle that salvation is conditional. Ever since that early period, then, when the issue was being examined again, Arminians have taught that those who are truly saved need to be warned against apostasy as a real and possible danger.

Key to this belief is the conviction that salvation is conditional. In that case, continuing to possess salvation is continuing to meet the biblical condition of faith. It is true that Arminians of different times and places have presented the details of this view in different ways. Even so, this view most certainly does *not* require thinking that salvation (whether at first or subsequently) is by works in any sense.

The Arminian believes, with the Calvinist, that the Bible warns the regenerate against turning away from God: in other words, against apostasy. It seems clear to the Arminian, then, that the possibility of apostasy must therefore really exist.

Among matters that are debated by Arminians within their own ranks are such questions as the following.

---

[3]Arminius, II:502-03.
[4]Arminius, III:491ff.

•*Does the word "elect" include only those who per-severe to final salvation, or does it include those who are regenerated and fall away?* Arminius himself defined election so as to favor the first of these two pos-sibilities. In this way, he apparently agreed with Augustine, that the regenerate who apostatize are non-elect.[5] This issue may be as much a matter of terminolo-gy as anything else. It will not be pursued in this work.

•*Can apostasy be remedied?* In other words, can one who is regenerate and becomes unregenerate via apostasy be regenerated again? There have been Arminians on both sides of this question. Again, the details of this difference will not be explored at length in this work. I think it is clear that the answer is no, and some reasons for this will be indicated in chapter two, as the message of the book of Hebrews is expounded.

## The Scriptural Argument for Conditional Perseverance

The Arminian is quick to urge that the issue of whether a saved person may be lost should be settled not on systematic but on biblical grounds. That is (as all would agree) the question: Does the Bible teach the pos-sibility of apostasy?

### New Testament Passages

New Testament passages teaching the possibility of apostasy include the following.

1. *The book of Hebrews as a whole.* Warnings and exhortations relative to apostasy and perseverance are thematic throughout the book. Each main section has a

---

[5] See Arminius' discussion in III:511, for example.

hortatory "center" assuming the possibility of apostasy. These are:

- chs. 1, 2, with 2:1-4 at the heart;
- chs. 3, 4, with 3:7—4:2 at the heart;
- chs. 5-7, with 5:11—6:12 at the heart, especially 6:4-6;
- chs. 8-12, with 10:19-39 and 12:1-24 at the heart.

Especially do the sections 6:4-6 and 10:19-39 take this doctrine to its fullest and clearest development. Without expanding on this now, I will simply refer to the following chapter, which will explore the teaching of Hebrews on this subject in detail. As will be noted there, if one wishes to get the best biblical material on any subject, he needs to consult the Bible where it is dealing directly with that subject, if this is possible. The book of Hebrews deals directly with perseverance and apostasy and provides the most important part of any biblical discussion of the subject.[6]

2. *Second Peter 2:18-22* is very similar to the passages that are at the heart of the book of Hebrews. This will also be treated in the following chapter, although somewhat more briefly than Hebrews.

3. *Other passages* are often included in such a discussion as this, and will be mentioned here just briefly. My own approach to the subject is such that I do not tend to look for intimations of the possibility of apostasy everywhere in the New Testament, but instead to build the case on the passages that treat the matter directly. Following that, I am prepared for other intimations of the possibility when they arise. Among these are the following.

---

[6] I would also refer the reader to Grant R. Osborne, "Soteriology in the Epistle to the Hebrews," in *Grace Unlimited* (Minneapolis: Bethany Fellowship, 1975), 144-61.

a. First Timothy 1:18-20 and 2 Timothy 2:16-18 refer to some, by name, who evidently apostatized from the faith.

b. Colossians 1:21-23 presents final salvation as conditional upon continuing in faith.

c. First Peter 1:5 indicates that our keeping, like our original justification, while it is by the powerful work of God, is also by faith.

d. Galatians 5:1-4 warns about falling from grace and apparently implies that this had happened to false teachers troubling the Galatians.

e. First Thessalonians 3:5; Philippians 2:16; and Galatians 4:9-11 can be grouped together as places where Paul referred to the frightening possibility that his work (which produced true believers) would come to be vain.

f. First Corinthians 10:1-14 warns those who consider (apparently correctly) that they stand against falling, using Israel as a telling example.

Many will use other passages that vary in strength (and applicability) on this subject. I for one am willing to stake the doctrine on the teaching of Hebrews and 2 Peter and then let the other passages confirm what we learn there. If those two books teach that apostasy really is possible, and I am confident they do, then the Calvinist is mistaken on this doctrine.

*Response to Calvinists' Scriptures*

Response to Scriptures prized by Calvinists as teaching the necessary (for sub-Calvinists,[7] unconditional) perseverance of the regenerate. These include:

*John 10:27-29:* "I give [my sheep] eternal life, and they shall never perish; neither shall anyone snatch them out of My hand."

*Romans 11:29:* "For the gifts and calling of God are irrevocable."

*Philippians 1:6:* "Being confident of this very thing, that He who has begun a good work in you will complete it until the day of Jesus Christ."

*Second Thessalonians 3:3:* "The Lord is faithful, who will establish you and guard you from the evil one."

*Second Timothy 1:12; 4:18:* "I know whom I have believed and am persuaded that he is able to keep what I have committed to Him until that Day." "And the Lord will deliver me from every evil work and preserve me for His heavenly kingdom."

*First Peter 1:5:* "Who are kept by the power of God through faith for salvation ready to be revealed in the last time."

*Romans 8:29, 30, 35-39:* "Whom he foreknew, He also predestined to be conformed to the image of His Son . . . Moreover whom He predestined, these He also called; whom He called, these He also justified; and whom He justified, these He also glorified."

1. Those passages, especially in the gospel of John, which contain strong promises of (final) salvation to believers and are therefore thought to imply necessary perseverance cannot be used for that purpose lest they "prove too much." In other words, to say that those promises require the impossibility of a changed situation

---

By "sub-Calvinists" I mean those who popularly hold the doctrine often termed "once saved, always saved" even though they are not truly Calvinistic. By this term I mean no opprobrium, only that they are less than fully developed Calvinists; they usually agree wth us who are Arminian on all points except the doctrine of perseverance.

places too great a burden on the syntax of the statements. And this can quickly be seen by comparing similar promises, using the very same syntax, to unbelievers. For example:

John 5:24
He that believes . . .
*shall not*
come into
condemnation.

John 3:36
He that believes not . . .
*shall not*
see life.

Grammatically, if the first means that the condition of the believer *cannot* be changed, then the second means that the condition of the unbeliever likewise *cannot* be changed. In fact, neither passage is even speaking to that issue. The unbeliever can leave his unbelief, become a believer, and see life—thus escaping from the promise made to the unbeliever who continues in his unbelief. Likewise, the believer can leave his belief, become an unbeliever, and come into condemnation—thus escaping from the promise made to believers who continue in faith. Each promise applies with equal force to those who continue in the respective state described.

As a believer, I know that I will not come into condemnation and rejoice in the Lord's promise.

2. Furthermore, as additional clarification of this point, one must note that in the overwhelming majority of passages like these, the "believing" is consistently presented as a progressive action (present tense in Greek). Thus, for example:

*John 3:36*—"The one who is *believing* (present participle) has eternal life."

*John 5:24*—This is precisely the same as 3:36.

8

*John 3:16*—". . . that everyone who is *believing* (present participle) may be having (present subjunctive) eternal life." One notes that the "having" corresponds precisely with the "believing."

3. In some passages, even though the conditionality of salvation is not explicitly stated, that conditionality is implicit and to be assumed from the other passages which do teach it clearly. (Throughout Scripture, most of God's dealings with men assume this conditionality, although it is sometimes and sometimes not stated.)

In this way John 10:27-29 is to be treated. The promise that "they shall never perish" is for those who are His sheep. It assumes that they remain His sheep. In fact, it is the same kind of promise as those mentioned above in point 1. Arminius observed, on this passage, that "unless the sheep are in the hands of the shepherd, they can not be safe against Satan," and went on to argue that if the sheep's defection precedes seizure by Satan the passage cannot be effectively used to prove unconditional safety.[8] (This passage also belongs in the category to follow.)

4. Some passages aim to assure us of our "security" from the forces that are against us. They do not mean to provide security against the consequences or possibilities of our own neglect, indifference, or unbelief.

As just noted, John 10:27-29 belongs in this category; the emphasis is that "no one is able to snatch them from My Father's hand." Satan himself cannot take us out of God's preservation.

So does Romans 8:35-39: none of the enemies listed in verses 38, 39 can separate us from God's love in Christ.

---

[8]Arminius, III:499.

5. Passages that express confidence, for the writer or his readers, that "God will perfect the work He has begun" in them are expressing confidence in what God will do, from His side, assuming that the persons spoken about continue in faith.

This applies to Philippians 1:6 and 2 Thessalonians 3:3, for example, where Paul's readers are referred to; and to 2 Timothy 1:12; 4:18 where Paul refers to himself.

6. While it is true that 1 Peter 1:5 expresses confidence in God's power as the means of keeping, it also indicates in the same breath that faith is the condition the regenerate must meet for God's keeping power to be effectively applied to them. In fact, this verse is stronger for the Arminian position than for that of the Calvinist.

7. Romans 8:29, 30 present the unbroken chain of calling-justification-glorification as the picture of what happens for those in whom God's purpose is fully accomplished, without even discussing the question whether any condition is required for any part of it to be accomplished. Regardless, "those whom He foreknew" still "conditions" the whole. Logically, the foreknowledge precedes the predestination. The identity of the ones involved here, as personally foreknown by God, is first settled. Then predestination (foreordination) proceeds from that and speaks of God's purpose for those already foreknown as His. Arminius offered the helpful suggestion that "foreknew" means both "whom He previously loved and affectionately regarded as His own" and that He knew in advance their "faith in Christ," since "the former cannot be true without the latter."[9]

---

[9]Arminius, III:313-14.

The point, then, is that God's final will for those whom He has come to know as believers is accomplished only in those who continue in faith. Their final salvation is as conditional as their initial salvation.

8. Romans 11:29 simply assures us that God is no "Indian giver" and cannot be thwarted in what He purposes to accomplish. Whatever else it may mean (which need not be pursued here), it is not in a context of personal-evangelical salvation as such.

## The Systematic Argument

Generally speaking, Arminians do not rely so much on logical arguments as do Calvinists—that is, not in support of this particular doctrine. (Indeed, Arminians have not traditionally been as strong for systematic theology.) Even so, like the Calvinist, the Arminian will insist that the view that apostasy is possible makes sense when linked with other soteriological doctrines. If God truly desires that all be saved, and sent Christ to atone for the sins of all, and "draws" all who hear with intelligence thus restoring their "freedom" to believe or reject the gospel, and then saves only those who freely choose to believe, then it follows that salvation is conditional.

And if salvation is conditional, then it really is conditional. As Arminius expressed the basic truth, "[God] embraces no one in Christ, unless he is in Christ. But no one is in Christ, except by faith in Christ, which is the necessary means of our union with Christ. If any one falls from faith, he falls from that union, and consequently, from the favor of God by which he was previously embraced in Christ."[10] He goes on to caution that

[10]Arminius, III:498.

11

the regenerate cannot fall from being embraced in Christ "while they continue to be believers, because so long they are in Christ."[11]

All this means, simply, from the Arminian perspective, that one's possession of salvation is, at any time, conditioned on faith. In the final analysis, then, the Arminian can rely only on whether the Scripture teaches this.

Logical or not, there are some who agree with Arminians on all the rest of the soteriological doctrines but disagree about perseverance; I call them "sub-Calvinists." In other words, they seem to believe that salvation is conditional, but they do not follow through with insistence that it remains conditional after the initial experience of regeneration.

Both for consistent Calvinists and for Arminians, that position seems to be internally contradictory. For that reason, I do not desire to pursue treatment of that position at length. I will therefore suggest, just briefly, a few responses (in addition to those already given) to some of the "logical" arguments which sub-Calvinists often make. They appear to enjoy such observations as these:

- One who has been born again can not be unborn.
- God is not an "Indian giver": He will not forgive and then take it back.
- When saved, a person is forgiven for past, present, and future sins.
- God will not allow a child of His, loved by Him, to perish.
- One born again will not desire to depart from God.

---

[11]Arminius, III:499.

- If a believer could be lost, the body of Christ would be maimed.
- One's child can never cease to be his child, regardless.

1. Some of these arguments are based on analogy and do not stand up under closer examination. For example, if the apostasy of a true believer meant that Christ's "body" would be "maimed," one wonders whether it is deformed until the last person in history is saved. Christ's body is not a physical thing to be presented in such terms.

2. Some of the arguments are based on logical, rather than biblical, statements about what God or a truly regenerate person would do, assuming that parallels with human experience can be applied. I readily want to believe that a regenerate person would not ever want to turn from God, in view of his new nature. But then I remember Adam and Eve, who did not even have a depraved nature to incline them toward sin within and fell by external temptation alone. And then I am not so smug about what I am and am not capable of.

3. Some of the arguments are mere words. While I suppose it is true that one cannot be "unborn" (which intentionally paints a ridiculous picture), he can certainly *die*.

To repeat, then, all such arguments ultimately trace back to the underlying assumption that salvation is not conditional. If it is, all the things God or man "would" do flow from that. In the final analysis, God is no more unloving to condemn a former child of His than any other of His creatures. He loves them all, but His saving relationship to them is conditioned by faith.

# Cautions About Developing a Doctrine of Apostasy

If the Bible teaches that apostasy from a truly regenerate state is possible, one must still be very cautious about expressing or formulating such a view. Here are some of the things to be careful about.

1. It is extremely important to express our view in such a way that faith, and not works, is the sole condition of salvation. We must not establish salvation by grace through faith with the right hand and take it away with the left.

The door out swings on the same hinges as the door in. In other words, the condition of salvation is always the same. As Arminius expressed this, it is "impossible for believers, as long as they remain believers, to decline from salvation."[12] If one gains access to saving grace by faith and not by works, he departs by unbelief and not by works.

It is important to understand the nature of saving faith. It carries absolutely no merit and stands as the opposite of works throughout the New Testament. As J. I. Packer has affirmed, "Faith is a matter first and foremost of looking outside and away from oneself to Christ and his cross as the sole ground of present forgiveness and future hope."[13] Once a person exercises faith in Christ and is converted, the nature of saving faith does not change. It remains, as before, the holding out of empty hands to God to accept His free gift, the deliber-

---

[12]Arminius, I:281. For evidence and citations showing that Thomas Grantham, an early General Baptist theologian, also made this clear, see Matthew Pinson, "The Diversity of Arminian Soteriology" (unpublished paper), 12-13.

[13]J. I. Packer, *What Did the Cross Achieve?* (Theological Students Fellowship, n.d., booklet reprinted from Tyndale Bulletin 25 [1974]), 30.

ate turning away from reliance in anything one can "do" and casting everything on what God, in Christ, has done.

"Saved by faith and kept by works" simply will not accord with biblical teaching relative to the basis of salvation. That basis always remains the same.

2. In whatever ways the positive "works" of a believer are involved in perseverance, we must relate them to faith and not as conditions of continuing in salvation as such. Expressing this relationship precisely is sometimes difficult; the Bible itself does not always attempt to make sure we understand that such things are not "essential" to salvation.

One cannot doubt that faithfulness, right conduct, prayer, and obedience to God are required of Christians, or that they are important for the Christian's spiritual well-being—and thus eventually for his perseverance. Even so, these must apparently be understood as integrally related to the faith which is alone the condition of salvation. In other words, these "works"—if that is the right word—are evidences of faith (for the Christian, perhaps even means of strengthening or sustaining faith), but it is the faith and not the evidences of it that saves.

In that sense, we may even call them "essential," just as bearing apples is "essential" to an apple tree but *manifests* what the tree is instead of *making* the tree what it is.

3. Conversely (and equally difficult to express precisely sometimes), we must not make sinful acts, in themselves, the cause of falling from grace. Likewise we must not give the impression that every time a saved person sins he is lost and needs saving again. Furthermore we must not make the mistake of implying that saved people do not sin.

If faith is the condition for salvation, then unbelief is the "condition" for apostasy. Again then works have an important role, whether negatively or positively, but as evidences of faith and unbelief rather than as the fundamental condition of being saved or lost. As Scot McKnight puts it, although somewhat awkwardly, "The only sin . . . capable of destroying a genuine believer's faith is the sin of apostasy."[14] Better to say that the retraction of faith is the only, final means of apostasy; apostasy is a willful retraction of faith.

Do Christians sin? Most assuredly so. Even Wesleyan Arminians who believe in some form of "entire sanctification" believe Christians sin. So do Calvinists, although the classical Calvinists do not encourage us to think that Christians go on indefinitely in lives characterized by sin. What, then, is the difference between the sins of a regenerate person and those of someone unregenerate?

While I am cautious enough to know that I cannot always examine the life of an individual and make a dogmatic judgment about his condition, I think I can define the fundamental difference involved. When an unsaved person sins, that sin represents what he really is by nature. When a regenerate person sins, that sin is a contradiction of what he really is, and he recognizes it as such. Consequently, in the loosely quoted words of 1 John 3:7, the regenerate person does not live in sin; the unregenerate person does. But in both cases the practice is evidence of the inner nature, not its cause.

We rejoice that God, who makes the only judgment that counts, knows perfectly the heart of each individ-

---

[14]Scot McKnight, "The Warning Passages of Hebrews: A Formal Analysis and Theological Conclusions" (*Trinity Journal* 13NS [1992]), 55.

ual, whether genuine faith is there. We, on the other hand, can "judge" only by what can be seen on the outside, and that kind of judgment—even though it must often be made—may be wrong. In biblical terms, then, we will rightly continue to regard any person whose life is characterized by sinful practice (regardless what he claims about "salvation") as having no grounds for assurance of salvation.

Does any of this mean that whenever I sin I must immediately doubt my salvation? No. And here we ought to be sure that our way of framing this doctrine provides for God's chastisement. According to Hebrews 12:3-15, God chastises His children when they sin because He loves them as His children. This makes clear that one may do wrong and be chastised for it as a child of God.

4. Corollary to what has already been said, we must allow in our expression of this doctrine for the fact that the saving works of grace we receive are based on "union with Christ" and that union is established on meeting the condition of faith. I receive such soteriological blessings as justification—my righteous standing before God in the righteousness of Jesus Christ—by virtue of being "in Him."

If the righteousness of Christ is imputed to me "in Christ," then that status is mine so long as I am in Him. And if I am in Him by faith, then only by a forsaking of saving faith will I be "out of" Him—as crude as that sounds. (While this statement is "logically" expressed, I see no alternative to it when I grapple with the New Testament teaching about the meaning and condition of justification.)

One of the implications of this is, simply, that there is no state "in between" being saved and lost—no

Protestant "purgatory" in this life or the next. Any given individual, at any time, is either in saving union with Christ or not. And if he is in Christ, he is by faith alone. Nor does physical death itself bring about any change in one's justified or unjustified state (although, of course, one's state might change very close to the point of death). At the same time, "dying in sin" is certainly a biblical expression that refers to being lost.

5. It is important, therefore, for us who believe in the possibility of apostasy to teach assurance of salvation and the proper grounds for that assurance. This viewpoint does not mean, for example, that one may not have assurance, or that one must go about as though walking on eggshells for fear of "losing" his salvation. Living in fear or with lack of assurance of salvation is neither God's will for His child nor in harmony with biblical teaching.

Assurance, therefore, must be based on the Word of God, which promises salvation to those who turn away from their works and put faith in Jesus Christ. Confirming that assurance for those who do this will be the inner testimony of the Spirit of God. Understanding that being accounted righteous before God depends on the righteousness of Christ imputed to the one in Him by faith should help the most timid believer have assurance of salvation.

At the same time, the Bible offers us no encouragement to provide assurance of salvation to those whose lives are characterized by sinful practice. Both traditional Calvinists and Arminians will agree with this.

6. Also important, we must express our view in such a way that apostasy is recognized as a serious and willful, decisive crisis. Apostasy is not what most people

mean by "backsliding." It is not something that a true believer, regenerated by the Spirit of God, can do lightly and easily. One is not saved today, lost tomorrow, and saved again the day after.

So long as one continues to exercise saving faith, he has not committed apostasy. Indeed, it appears to be true that so long as one desires to be right with God in Christ he has not committed apostasy, but it is beyond my purpose here to explore that point.

Apostasy, apparently, cannot be reversed and is final. As already noted, I will provide grounds for this view in the following chapter. At the same time, while apostasy is not easily arrived at, we ought not to say that it does not really happen. Both in the Bible and in the experiential observation of the church, cases of apostasy are relatively common.

7. It is equally important, therefore, for us to warn believers about the danger of apostasy and to exhort them to persevere in faith and good works, not as a means of frightening or troubling them but as a means of edifying them and nurturing their spiritual development, which is the one, sure, biblical way of avoiding apostasy (2 Peter 3:17, 18).

As already noted, the traditional Calvinist agrees that the New Testament itself does actually present such warnings and exhortations, and that these are in fact means of perseverance. It is obviously biblical, therefore, to take up such warnings and exhortations. It is not so obviously biblical, however, to teach believers that these are merely warnings against something that cannot really happen. One wonders if these warnings and exhortations can have their intended effect if the presenter afterward assures his hearers that such apostasy is not a real possibility. Do any of those pastors who deny the possibility of apostasy warn their flock against it?

If not, that is most certainly not the biblical way. Indeed, such warnings and exhortations have force precisely because they refer to a real danger. To convince believers that there is no possibility of apostasy is to negate the biblical warning. I cannot avoid saying, therefore, that the Calvinist attempt to explain the biblical warnings as means by which the perseverance is ensured is, finally, a sad travesty.

On the negative side, believers ought to be warned against those roads that might lead to apostasy. These will include tolerance of false doctrine, continued indulgence in sin, and rebelling against God's chastisement. Any of these may put one on a path that leads to the conscious and willful disbelief that is involved in "departing from the living God" (Hebrews 3:12).

On the positive side, believers ought to be exhorted and nurtured in spiritual development. As already noted, the entire epistle of 2 Peter presents this as the one way to be sure that one will not apostatize.

# For Further Reading on the Arminian Doctrine of Perseverance

Arminius, James. *The Writings of James Arminius* (three vols.), tr. James Nichols and W. R. Bagnall. Grand Rapids: Baker, 1956 (vol. I, pp. 252-255, 262-264, 278-282, 285-289; vol. II, pp. 499-501).

Duty, Guy. *If Ye Continue.* Minneapolis: Bethany Fellowship, 1966.

Forlines, F. Leroy. *Biblical Systematics.* Nashville: Randall House Publications, 1975 (pp. 207-230). [A colleague of this writer]

Marshall, I. Howard. *Kept By the Power of God.* Minneapolis: Bethany Fellowship, 1969.

Osborne, Grant. "Soteriology in the Epistle to the Hebrews" (ch. 8) and "Exegetical Notes on Calvinist Texts" (ch. 9), *Grace Unlimited,* ed. Clark H. Pinnock. Minneapolis: Bethany Fellowship, 1975. [Osborne does not seem to be as much in pursuit of novelty as do some of the other writers in this book, like Lake and Pinnock.]

Shank, Robert. *Life in the Son.* Springfield, Mo.: Westcott Publishers, 1960. [Shank believes that an apostate can be saved again.]

Watson, Richard. *Theological Institutes.* New York: Nelson and Phillips, 1850 (vol. II, pp. 295-301). [An important, early Wesleyan theologian.]

# CHAPTER TWO

# Hebrews, Second Peter, and the Possibility of Apostasy

It seems clear to me that a truly biblical or exegetical theology approach will sustain the doctrine I have set forth in the previous chapter. It is the purpose of this chapter to demonstrate this from Hebrews and Second Peter.

## Hebrews 6:4-6

For those who believe in the possibility of personal apostasy, the book of Hebrews as a whole and Hebrews 6:4-6 in particular is one of the most important passages involved in providing a biblical basis for the view. The greater part of this chapter, therefore, is devoted to a thorough exegesis of this key passage in the context of the book and to treat questions about how it relates to the possibility that a truly regenerate person may "fall from grace."

Whether they can agree on this doctrine or not, all Christians should agree that our teaching on any subject ought to be based on what the Bible has to say rather than on traditional, philosophical, or theological arguments. My aim here, then, is to determine exactly what Hebrews 6:4-6 teaches.

### The Context for the Passage

One of the requirements of good exegesis is to understand how a given passage fits into its context. In this case we should consider the general thrust of Hebrews as a whole. These three verses come in the midst of a book that has perseverance for its major theme.

We need not review the discussion about the original writer of Hebrews. The inspired text does not identify him or her.

Nor are we required to establish, for sure, the identity of the original audience. The inspired text does not tell us that either; the title "To the Hebrews" is a later addition.

Even so, the tradition that the "epistle" was written for Jewish Christians owes its strength to the obvious fact that all its teaching is presented against the backdrop of Jewish ritual. Kent is correct in saying, "Most conservatives would agree that the Hebrew-Christian character of Hebrews is self-evident."[1] He explains the usual understanding of the first readers' situation at the time:

---

[1] Homer A. Kent, *The Epistle to the Hebrews: A Commentary* (Grand Rapids: Baker, 1972), 23.

A careful study of the five warning passages shows their problem to have been the very serious one of wavering before the temptation to leave the Christian movement and retire to the safer haven of Judaism. By such a move, they could avoid persecution from their Jewish kinsmen, and also enjoy the legal protection which Judaism had from the government—a boon which Christians at this time [in the sixties] did not possess.[2]

Even if that conclusion were successfully challenged (and there are some who would do so), the interpretation of the passage would not be significantly affected. Whoever the original readers were, an inductive study of Hebrews by itself makes clear that the readers were considering defection and in need of exhortation to persevere in the faith.

## A Theme of Hebrews

One indication of the dominant motif in Hebrews is the frequent occurrence of words urging the readers to hold to the faith. Several of these reflect the Greek root *ech-o*. In 2:1, the King James says, "We ought to give the more earnest heed to the things which we have heard." The word translated "give heed" is *prosech-o*, meaning "hold on to." In 3:6 we are said to make up Christ's house if we "hold fast"—a good translation of *katech-o*. The same word appears again in 3:14, "We have become partakers of Christ if we hold fast; and in 10:23, where we are exhorted to "hold fast." In 4:14 a different

---

[2] Kent, 25.

and even more forceful word occurs, *krate-o*, which means to cling to, seize, grasp. We are urged there to "cling to" our profession—to hold on for dear life.

Some writers have cited "let us go on" (6:1) as the key phrase of Hebrews; Griffith Thomas even used this as the name for his commentary.[3] Shank has correctly observed that "let us hold fast" is much more frequent and significant, far more deserving of status as the theme of the book.[4]

### *The Structure of Hebrews*

More important than this recurring theme-phrase is the pattern of the contents of Hebrews. An exhortation to persevere is at the heart of every major section of the book.

Almost everyone will agree that Hebrews gives its consuming interest to convincing the readers that Christ and the New Covenant are (1) infinitely superior to all that went before and (2) final. This Christological center of interest is certainly the doctrinal passion of the book. But the hortatory concern is perseverance. Indeed, almost the only practical exhortation contained in the whole book, except for brief miscellaneous exhortations in the concluding chapter, is the exhortation to persevere. As Osborne observes, "The willful apostasy of some from the faith" is "the particular problem to which the epistle is addressed."[5]

This concern for perseverance, inseparably linked with warnings against apostasy, is therefore the domi-

---

[3]W. H. Griffith Thomas, *Let Us Go On* (Grand Rapids: Zondervan, 1944).

[4]Robert Shank, *Life in the Son* (Springfield, Mo.: Westcott Publishers, 1960), 233.

[5]Grant R. Osborne, "Soteriology in the Epistle to the Hebrews," in *Grace Unlimited*, ed. Clark Pinnock (Minneapolis: Bethany Fellowship, 1975), 146.

nant pastoral concern of Hebrews. It makes up the very warp and woof of it, the pattern about which all the cloth is woven. Even the teaching about the superiority and finality of revelation and religion in Christ serves as reenforcement for the repeated pleas to "hold fast to the faith." Guthrie comments, "The writer has no intention of writing a purely academic treatise, but aims throughout to emphasize the practical significance of the points he makes."[6] Marshall notes that the warning passages "are not parentheses ... but form an integral part of the structure in which dogmatic theology and practical exhortations are intricately bound up together."[7]

Hebrews is not merely an "epistle" in the usual sense of the word. In form, it closes like one but does not begin like one. In content, it is more like a full-length sermon. Thus Buchanan's comment that Hebrews "is a homiletical midrash based on Ps 110."[8] (But this gives the "sermon" too narrow a scope.) The text and introduction to this sermon appear in 1:1, 2: God has spoken in various ways in the past, but has given His final and perfect word to us in His Son. The conclusion appears in 12:25-29—You must not refuse Him who speaks; if those who refused Him when He spoke in the past did not escape, much more we will not escape if we turn away from the one who is His final Word. This conclusion makes clear the point of the whole message, which 13:22 calls a "word of exhortation."

---

[6]Donald Guthrie, *Hebrews*, Tyndale NT Commentaries (Downers Grove: Inter-Varsity, 1983), 81.

[7]I. Howard Marshall, *Kept By the Power of God* (Minneapolis: Bethany Fellowship, 1969), 139.

[8]George Wesley Buchanan, "To The Hebrews," *Anchor Bible* (New York: Doubleday, 1972), xix.

The first section of Hebrews (after the introduction in 1:1-5) is generally agreed to be chapters 1 and 2, which Westcott entitles "The Superiority of the Son, the Mediator of the New Revelation, to Angels."[9] At the heart of this is 2:1-4 (Kent's "First Warning Passage"). Verse 1 literally reads, "Because of this, it is necessary for us to be holding on all the more exceedingly to the things heard, lest haply we drift away (from them)." Even those who do not believe that personal apostasy is possible agree that the meaning really is, lest we drift or slip away: "The meaning of the word and its personal subject ("we") indicate not that something might drift away from us, but that 'we' might drift away from something."[10] The word was sometimes used for a boat that had slipped its moorings.

The second section is clearly chapters 3 and 4: "Moses, Joshua, Jesus—the Founders of the Old Economy and of the New."[11] At the heart of this is the passage 3:7—4:2 (Kent's "Second Warning Passage," which he extends to 4:13). There we read, literally: "Be on watch, brothers, lest haply there will be in anyone of you a wicked, unbelieving heart in departing from the living God" (3:12). "Departing" is the very Greek root that our English "apostasy" comes from (the verb *apostenai;* the cognate noun is *apostasia*), "an unbelief which abandons hope."[12] The writer is saying, simply, "Brothers, be on guard against apostatizing from God."

[9] B. F. Westcott, *The Epistle to the Hebrews* (Grand Rapids: Eerdmans, 1955), xlviii.

[10] Kent, 47.

[11] Westcott, xlviii.

[12] *Theological Dictionary of the New Testament* (Grand Rapids: Eerdsmans, 1972, here- after identified as TDNT), I:513.

Lenski notes that unbelief in Hebrews "is thus understood in the sense of once having believed in the living God and then having turned away from him."[13] Bruce compares "the action of the Israelites when they 'turned back in their hearts unto Egypt'. . . a gesture of outright apostasy, a complete break with God."[14] Guthrie sees in this "the greatest defection possible."[15]

We also read in this section, literally, "We have come to be partakers of Christ, if in fact we hold fast [the theme word discussed above] the beginning of our confidence firm unto the end" (3:14). Westcott comments, "That which has been stated as fact [that is, having become partakers of Christ] is now made conditional in its permanence on the maintenance of faith."[16]

The third and central section is chapters 5-7: "The Highpriesthood of Christ, Universal and Sovereign."[17] At the heart of this is the extended exhortation of 5:11—6:12 (Kent's "Third Warning Passage," 5:11—6:20). Since this is the passage that contains 6:4-6, further comment is saved for the next part of this chapter.

The final section is chapters 8-12, although many interpreters prefer to make this into two sections, 8:1—10:18 and 10:19—12:29. If I were going to divide this into two main parts, I would divide at 11:1; then each of the teaching parts would be concluded with exhortation. But this matter does not need to occupy us here.

---

[13] R. C. H. Lenski, *The Interpretation of the Epistle to the Hebrews and The Epistle of James* (Minneapolis: Augsburg, 1966), 118.

[14] F. F. Bruce, *The Epistle to the Hebrews* (New International Commentary of the NT: Grand Rapids: Eerdmans, 1964), 66.

[15] Guthrie, 106.

[16] Westscott, 85.

[17] Westcott, xlix.

Regardless, there are two extended passages of exhortation woven into these five chapters. Kent's "Fourth Warning Passage" is 10:26-31; actually the exhortation extends from 10:10-39. Once again we are urged, literally, "Let us be holding fast [the theme word again] the confession of hope unwavering" (10:23). And to this is attached the terrible warning of verses 26-31: if we will to take back up our sinful ways, thus trampling under foot Christ's blood and doing insult to the Spirit, our punishment will be much worse than death without mercy as prescribed in the Mosaic economy.

Citing the favorite text for justification by faith, "The just shall live by faith," the writer adds (from the same source in the LXX), "but if he [the just one] draws back, my soul has no pleasure in him" (verse 38). Westcott correctly urges that it is altogether unwarranted to read the inserted "any man" of the King James as though this is someone other than "the just one."[18] The inspired writer of Hebrews is referring, specifically, to the "drawing back" of one justified by faith, leading to this pronouncement by God.

The final, extensive exhortation serves as the conclusion to the section and to the "sermon" as a whole and includes all of chapter 12 (although Kent includes, in his "Fifth Warning Passage," just 12:18-29). Here we are warned "lest anyone fall back from [Westcott: "implying a moral separation"[19]] the grace of God" (verse 15). The writer backs this up with the example of Esau as one for whom no place of repentance and restoration to what he had lost could be found. The serious conclusion, then,

---

[18]Westcott, 337.
[19]Westcott, 406.

is that we will not escape if we "turn back from" the One who is, and who speaks, from heaven. Actually, the writer does not present this in a merely hypothetical manner; literally, the words are "we who are turning back from." He evidently regards the process of apostasy as having already begun and identifies himself with his people in this awful thing.

It is clear, then, that 6:4-6 is at the heart of a book that has the question of apostasy and perseverance at its very roots. The five warning passages tie the "sermon" together and reveal that its main thrust is to exhort the audience to hold fast to the faith they have placed in Christ lest apostasy occur, lest they forsake the very One God has revealed as providing, by His redemptive work, room for them to stand righteous before God. There is no sacrifice for sins, no provision for righteousness, outside Him.

Such is the context of 6:4-6, and it is clear that each of the five warning passages is clarified by the other warning passages. All five describe the same sin, include the same warning, and exhort the same audience. This fact has been conclusively demonstrated by Scot McKnight in a study that clearly establishes the meaning of each of these components by a "synthetic" comparison of the passages.[20]

### The Text

To begin, here is my own more or less literal translation of the passage, arranged so that the reader can more clearly see the relationship of the clauses:

---

[20]Scot McKnight, "The Warning Passages of Hebrews: A Formal Analysis and Theological Conclusions" (*Trinity Journal* 13NS [1992]), 21-59.

> For it is impossible for those
>> who were once-for-all enlightened
>> and who tasted of the heavenly free gift
>> and who became partakers of the Holy Spirit
>> and who tasted God's good word and the
>>> powers of
>> the coming age
>> and who fell away
> to be being renewed again unto repentance,
> they crucifying again to/for themselves the Son of
> God and exposing (Him) to public shame.

The exegesis and interpretation of these words involve three key questions about the experience of the persons whom the writer is describing. (For the moment, this need not involve whether they had actually done all this or were simply candidates for it.)

## Does the Passage Describe Genuine Christians?

This question arises because some interpreters suggest that something less than genuine conversion is meant. The people that the writer of Hebrews describes are said to have experienced four positive things. The question, then, depends on the meaning of these four clauses, as follows.

*1. They were once-for-all enlightened.* This appears, by any reading, to refer to the spiritual enlightenment we associate with salvation. The verb *photizomai* means to give one light or bring him into light. The very same description appears again in 10:32, where also there is no reason to doubt that the writer consciously uses it to mean conversion. The biblical background involved is the contrast between darkness and light and between

32

those in the darkness and those in the light (cf. 2 Cor. 4:4).

The word translated "once," *hapax*, has the idea "once for all" or "once effectively." This same word occurs several times in Hebrews, and comparing them is instructive: 9:7, 26, 27, 28; 10:2; 12:26, 27. In all these places the word consciously implies something done once in a way that no repetition or addition is needed to complete it. Kent acknowledges that "The use of 'once for all' points to something complete, rather than partial or inadequate."[21]

*2. They tasted of the heavenly free gift.* Two points have sometimes been made against equating this with genuine salvation. One is the use of "taste," said by some to imply a partial rather than a full experience. But that objection reflects a modern English idiom rather than the way the ancient Greeks used *geuomai*. Even when referring to food, they could use this word for full-fledged eating, as in Acts 10:10. More important, they used this word metaphorically to mean "experience." Especially significant is the fact that the writer of Hebrews uses this very same word again in 2:9 to refer to Christ "experiencing" death. No one would wish to say that He only partially or incompletely experienced death.

The other objection is more technical: namely, that "taste" is followed here by a *genitive* object rather than by the accusative, and that the genitive case merely identifies what kind of thing it is while the accusative is the case of extent. The objectors say this means that the people referred to tasted of the gift rather than tasting to the full extent of experience.

---

[21]Kent, 108.

Two things are wrong with this objection. First, while the genitive does not expressly speak of extent, it does not deny it. More important, the genitive is also the case used for the object in 2:9 where Christ tasted death! (See also on the fourth clause, below.)

The people being described, then, "experienced" the heavenly free-gift. Interpreters are not unanimous in identifying this "free gift," but the disagreement is more technical than substantial, and the general meaning is clear. The various interpreters suggest salvation, eternal life, forgiveness of sins, the Holy Spirit, or Christ Himself. Probably the best conclusion is that it means salvation and what goes with it: justification and eternal life in Christ, "salvation blessings."[22]

*3. They became partakers of the Holy Spirit.* Guthrie observes, "The idea of sharing the Holy Spirit is remarkable. This at once distinguishes the person from one who has no more than a nodding acquaintance with Christianity."[23] The word "partakers," *metochoi*, which means "to have together with," is apparently used by the writer of Hebrews exclusively to refer to Christians' common participation in things related to their salvation. In 3:1 we are "partakers" of the heavenly calling; in 3:14 "partakers" of Christ; and in 12:8 "partakers" of the discipline that distinguishes between true sons and bastards. Either of these three, or the one here, will by itself be adequate to identify such a "partaker" as a Christian.

To have the Holy Spirit, in common with other believers, is certainly to be a Christian. Receiving the gift of the Spirit, in the New Testament, is a regular way of

---

[22] Osborne, 149.
[23] Guthrie, 142.

stating what it means to become a Christian. Acts 2:38, 39 and Galatians 3:14 are just two of many examples.

*4. They tasted God's good word and the powers of the coming age.* We meet "taste" again; see above on the second clause. If any doubt should remain about the fact that the genitive object was used in the clause above, this one will remove that doubt. The object is accusative here.

Those described have "experienced" God's good word. This means that they have experienced the goodness that God has spoken of. God has spoken good to those who put faith in Him, and these have experienced that good. As Kent puts it, this is "experiencing the word of God in the gospel and finding it good."[24] Compare 1 Peter 2:3.

Furthermore, they have "experienced" the powers of the coming age. "Powers," *dunameis,* often means "miracles" (as in 2:4). In its broadest sense, that is the idea here: supernatural workings. Manifestations of divine power do not have their origin in this present age. All the mighty works of God are from the age to come, "other-world power" as Lenski expresses it.[25] But Christians, though still living in the present age, have already begun to experience the supernatural workings characteristic of the age to come. This includes more than we need to discuss here, but regeneration and the gift of the Spirit are the initial powerful works of the age to come that all Christians have in common.

Osborne points out that "the age to come" is important in the eschatology of Hebrews, where "Eschatology

---

[24]Kent, 109.
[25]Lenski, 184.

becomes a part of soteriology" and so this phrase implies a foretaste of "kingdom blessings."[26] J. Behm, discussing all the "taste" clauses in the verse, says they describe "vividly the reality of personal experiences of salvation enjoyed by Christians at conversion."[27]

Of these four clauses as a whole, then, we may say that one would be hard put to find a better description of genuine regeneration and conversion. Either of them will stand by itself in this respect. The four together provide one of the finest statements about salvation, from its experiential side, that appears anywhere in the Scriptures.

Among those who apparently agree with the position taken here is Scot McKnight, who calls these "phenomenological-true believers," by which he means that they are genuine believers at present, in every way observable. The writer of Hebrews perceives them so. But they might or might not persevere in that faith. If they do, their faith is "saving" faith in the eyes of the writer of Hebrews, since he uses "salvation" to mean final salvation. Meanwhile, theirs is the condition of all believers in the present life.[28]

I must criticize McKnight's terminology in what is otherwise an outstanding monograph. Although he justifies this as a way of being true to the use of words like faith and salvation in Hebrews, I think he is at fault on several counts. (1) He seems not to realize how jarring are statements like, "This expression gives us even more evidence for contending that these readers were, at the phenomenological level, converts to Jesus Christ."[29] In

---

[26] Osborne, 148, 149.
[27] TDNT, I:676.
[28] McKnight, 24, 25.
[29] McKnight, 47.

fact, the statement would sound more like the writer of Hebrews if "at the phenomenological level" were omitted. (2) The "phenomenological" qualifier casts doubt on the genuineness of their Christianity, even though McKnight makes clear that he does not intend this, affirming that those referred to are "Christian" and "regenerate," and that the faith of all Christians is "phenomenological-true."[30] (3) It is confusing to use terms in ways different from their customary use. Nor does it soften the underlying disagreement with Calvinism—not that I suppose McKnight intended it to. (4) While we may not be able to judge the genuineness of faith on just an observable basis, God is not thus limited and the divine inspiration of the writer of Hebrews would apparently guarantee the genuineness of the faith of those he describes as genuine. In other words, then, there is finally no difference between a "phenomenological-true believer" and a "true believer" in the book of Hebrews.

## Does the Passage Describe Apostasy From Salvation?

The answer to this question resides in the meaning of the clause which the King James renders, "If they shall fall away."

There is not much dispute about the meaning of the words. In light of the impossibility of repentance attached (to be discussed below), most interpreters readily accept that to "fall away" as used here leaves a person outside a saving relationship with Christ.[31]

---

[30]McKnight, 49.

[31]An exception is T. K. Oberholtzer in a series, "The Warning Passages of Hebrews," in *Bibliotheca Sacra* 145, 146 (1988-89).

"Fall away" is *parapipt-o*, and this is the verb's only appearance in the New Testament. It occurs in the LXX in passages that also refer to apostasy, as Ezekiel 18:24. As Kent says, though he does not believe apostasy is possible, the words mean "complete and final repudiation of Christ (as in 10:26, 27)" and describe "those who are regenerated and then repudiate Christ and forsake Him."[32] The "falling away" is defection from the experience described in the four positive clauses that precede.

That is what apostasy means. In light of the contents of the entire book of Hebrews, as outlined above, the "falling away" is obviously synonymous with "drifting away" (2:1), "departing from [literally, apostatizing from] the living God" (3:12), "drawing back" (10:38), and "turning away from the One from heaven" (12:25). McKnight convincingly shows that the one "sin" of apostasy is in view throughout Hebrews.[33]

Some interpreters, perhaps unfamiliar with the Greek original, misunderstand the relationship of the clauses. They readily acknowledge that the first four, positive clauses describe a truly regenerate state. Then they add, using the King James wording, that such regenerate persons as these, if they should fall away, could not possibly be renewed to repentance. One notes the emphasis on the "if." In fact, they say, this is a purely hypothetical addition; the truly regenerate cannot really "fall away."

But the grammar of the original will not permit this reading. The fifth clause cannot be made a merely hypothetical attachment to an otherwise real set of circumstances. The literal translation I gave earlier shows this in

---

[32]Kent, 110.
[33]McKnight, 39, 40.

English. In Greek the grammar is equally clear. We have five equal, coordinate, aorist-tense participles in a series. The persons described have done all five things equally: they were enlightened, experienced the gift of God, became partakers of the Holy Spirit, experienced God's good word and the miraculous works of the age to come, and fell away.

That is exactly the way the Greek reads. I assume the King James translators introduced the "if" to make the long sentence smoother and more readable, at the same time omitting the Greek *kai* ("and"). Kent recognizes what is involved: "Grammatically there is no warrant for treating the last [participle] in the series any differently from the others."[34] The NASB gives an especially clear and accurate translation: "In the case of those who have once been enlightened ... and then have fallen away, it is impossible to renew them again to repentance." (Even the "then" is unnecessary and not in the original.)

## What Is the Nature of the Impossibility Referred To?

Of those who have experienced the five things listed, the writer says that it is not possible to be renewing them again to repentance. This affirmation is very strong. For emphasis the word "impossible" is moved up to the front of the whole sentence.

Two things are involved in this impossibility, although they cannot be separated. First, one must consider what is impossible. It is "renewal to repentance," which makes clear that they had repented earlier. Repentance is a thorough-going change of heart, mind,

[34]Kent, 108.

and will. Now that the falling away has taken place, repentance from that apostate unbelief is not possible. All this seems fairly obvious from the words themselves.

Repentance has already been introduced into the immediate context. In verses 1-3 the writer has said that we ought, in our experience, to let ourselves be carried along toward maturity rather than putting down again (among other things) the foundation of "repentance from dead works." For, he adds in verses 4-6, the person who is converted and falls away cannot be renewed unto repentance. Clearly, then, the same repentance is meant: the repentance from dead works that comes at conversion.

The association of "repentance" with a warning against apostasy in 12:15-17 strengthens this understanding. The warning "lest anyone fall back from the grace of God" is linked to the case of Esau for whom "a place (opportunity) of repentance was not found"—one that would enable him to receive the inheritance he had so tragically traded away.

The second consideration is *why* there is no possibility for repentance. The explanation is contained in the words (in the King James), "seeing they crucify to themselves the Son of God afresh, and put him to an open shame." The translators supplied "seeing"; the literal words are, "(they) re-crucifying to (or, for) themselves the Son of God and exposing (Him) to public shame." The cross, in Roman times, was an object of special shame. Apostates are "identified with those whose hatred of Christ led them to exhibit him as an object of contempt on a hated Roman gibbet."[35] Arminius faced William

---

[35]Guthrie, 144.

Perkins' objection to the possibility of apostasy on the grounds that "entire defection from true faith would require a second ingrafting, if indeed he, who falls away, shall be saved." One line of his response was, "It is not absolutely necessary that he, who falls away, should be again ingrafted; indeed some will say, from Heb. vi and x, that one, who wholly falls away from the true faith, can not be restored by repentance."[36] It is not clear whether this would have been the view of Arminius himself. It is clear that Thomas Grantham, the early General Baptist theologian, agreed that apostasy is "an 'irrevocable Estate' from which the apostate can never return."[37]

A very few interpreters would argue that this is not a reason at all and that the KJV translators made a poor choice of words when they used "seeing." The technicalities of the grammar are that these are circumstantial participles, which leaves it to the interpreter to determine from the context just what kind of circumstances are meant. Thus Shank offers his opinion that these are circumstances of time and not of cause (as in KJV). He would therefore translate thus: "It is impossible to renew them again to repentance so long as they are crucifying . . . and publicly shaming Him."[38]

Such a view leads to the conclusion that the apostasy described here can be remedied, that repentance from apostasy back to God is not finally impossible after all, so that the writer of Hebrews only means a tempo-

---

[36] James Arminius, *The Writings of James Arminius,* tr. James Nichols and W. R. Bagnall (Grand Rapids: Baker, 1956), III:494.

[37] Matthew Pinson, "The Diversity of Arminian Soteriology" (unpublished paper), 13, citing Thomas Grantham, *Christianismus Primitivus,* or the *Ancient Christian Religion* (London: Francis Smith, 1678), II:154.

[38] Shank, 318.

rary impossibility. Westcott (even though he, unlike Shank, takes the participles as causal) believes that the passage teaches apostasy and that the apostasy can be remedied: "The moral cause of the impossibility which has been affirmed . . . is an active, continuous hostility to Christ in the souls of such men."[39] He therefore limits the impossibility to human agency and suggests that divine agency can accomplish in such a case a restoration from death to life (technically not another new birth).[40] I agree with Marshall that "The passage gives us no right to assert that there may be a special intervention of God to restore those whom men cannot restore."[41]

Very few interpreters will accept that the apostasy described here can be remedied. There are several good arguments against it. For one thing, the clause simply does not fit as a temporal clause. It "feels right" only as causal and the interpreters and translators are nearly unanimous in rendering it, "It is impossible . . . because ("seeing") they are re-crucifying Him."

For another thing, the emphasis on the impossible, as noted above, makes more sense if this is a real (and not just a merely human) impossibility. Shank's interpretation winds up saying that it is impossible to renew them to repentance so long as they persist in their attitude of rejection—which is not much of a point since it is always impossible to bring anyone to repentance so long as he persists in rejection: "a truism hardly worth putting into words."[42] This almost amounts to saying that it is impossible to bring such a person to repentance so

[39]Westcott, 151.
[40]Westcott, 150, 165.
[41]Marshall, 142.
[42]Bruce, 124.

long as he persists in an attitude that makes it impossible to bring him to repentance; and that is pure tautology. Westcott's way of putting it is not quite that weak. What he is saying is that it is impossible for men to bring this person back to repentance because of his active, ongoing hostility to Christ. But that does not do justice to the sentence either; it is always impossible for men to produce repentance without divine agency.

Yet another thing: one must do justice to the point of verses 7, 8. The "for" in verse 7 attaches these two verses to verses 4-6 as a reason, given in the form of an illustration. Thus the impossibility of verses 4-6 lies not merely in the attitude of the apostate but also in the judgment of God. The land in the illustration is "reprobate land"[43]— *adokimos* (as in 1 Cor. 9:27, "castaway").

Finally, one more reason for regarding the apostasy of verses 4-6 as final is found in the other passages about apostasy in Hebrews, as listed earlier in this article. Thus 2:1-4 asks how we shall escape if we "drift away" from this great salvation, implying that there is no escape. The passage beginning at 3:7 backs up its warning against apostasy by reminding us of the Israelites to whom God swore that they would not enter the promised rest. In 12:25, again, the warning is that we will not escape if we turn away from Him.

Especially does 10:26-39 shed light on the serious finality of apostasy. This passage warns that God will take no pleasure in the one who draws back (verse 38). Bruce speaks of this as "the divine displeasure which will rest upon him."[44] The passage also provides us with

---

[43] Bruce, 124.
[44] Bruce, 274.

the true reason for the impossibility: for the one who wills to return to sin, thus treading under foot the blood of Christ's sacrifice for sin and insulting the Spirit of grace, there "remaineth no more sacrifice for sins." Christ's blood is the only atonement for sin. Having experienced and then rejected that, the apostate has nowhere else to turn. The re-crucifying and public exposure of Christ in 6:6 clearly refers to the same thing as the treading under foot and counting the atoning blood an unholy thing in 10:29.

For all these reasons, then, it seems clear that the apostasy of these verses is a final and irreversible apostasy.

## Other Readings of the Text

Briefly, and in summary fashion, notice should be taken of the views of those who disagree with the position taken here, whether Calvinists or sub-Calvinists. Among those who do not believe that personal apostasy from saving faith is possible, there are two main ways of explaining the meaning of Hebrews 6:4-6.

### Denial of Regeneration

The first is to say that the people described here were not meant to be pictured as truly regenerate. As Wuest expresses this view, the "apostasy" referred to in Hebrews is "the act of an unsaved Jew ... renouncing his professed faith in Messiah."[45] Bruce compares these to people "immunized against a disease by being inoculated with a mild form of it ... something which, for the

---

[45]Kenneth S. Wuest, "Hebrews Six in the Greek New Testament" (*Bibliotheca Sacra* 119 [1962]), 46.

time being, looks so like the real thing that it is genuinely mistaken for it.[46] Morris compares Simon Magus, quoting Acts 8:13, that he "believed and was baptized. And he followed Philip everywhere." Then he notes, "This is as definite as anything in Hebrews 6."[47] (In fact, everything in Hebrews 6:4, 5 is more definite than that!)

This approach has already been answered above and need not be discussed at length again. (One wishes to say that such exegesis serves the Calvinist's need to negate the Arminian view; one wonders, however, if it serves equally well as a basis for warning persons who are in such danger.) The fact is that the four positive participles describe, in the clearest way possible, genuine conversion. Even Kent has it precisely right when he says that he "doubts whether the same description if found elsewhere would ever be explained by these interpreters in any way other than full regeneration."[48] Nicole, after offering Calvinistic explanations of the fact that these apostates had earlier "repented," acknowledges that "neither of these explanations appears entirely free of difficulty, although one may prefer to have recourse to them rather than to be forced to the conclusion that regenerate individuals may be lost."[49] Good for his honesty, bad for his exegetical objectivity!

## *Hypothetical Warning*

The other approach is to say that the writer is dealing only with a hypothetical situation. I have noted ear-

---

[46]Bruce, 118, 119.

[47]Leon Morris, *Hebrews*, Bible Study Commentary (Grand Rapids: Zondervan, 1983), 59.

[48]Kent, 11.

[49]Roger Nicole, "Some Comments on Hebrews 6:4-6 and the Doctrine of the Perseverance of God with the Saints," in *Current Issues in Biblical and Patristic Interpretation,* ed. G. Hawthorne (Grand Rapids: Eerdsman, 1975), 361.

lier that it simply will not do to regard the first four participles as real and then treat the fifth as hypothetical. But some interpreters treat the entire description as hypothetical. In other words, they say that the passage really describes a truly regenerate person who commits apostasy. But, they say, such a case is hypothetical and cannot really occur.

This is Kent's view. He suggests that "The author has described a supposed case, assuming for the moment the presuppositions of some of his confused and wavering readers."[50] In other words, assuming that the readers as true Christians were being tempted to forsake Christianity and return to Judaism, the writer is showing them the folly of their consideration by saying that a person who was truly saved and forsook Christ could never again be saved. "True believers (seeing what an awful consequence apostasy would have, if it were possible) would be warned by this statement to remain firm (and from the human standpoint the warnings of Scripture are a means to ensure the perseverance of the saints)."[51]

Kent quotes Westcott for this explanation: "The case is hypothetical. There is nothing to show that the conditions of fatal apostasy had been fulfilled, still less that they had been fulfilled in the case of any of these addressed. Indeed the contrary is assumed: vv. 9ff."[52] But he is clearly mistaken in his reading of Westcott, who means something else entirely by "hypothetical." Westcott only means that the writer of Hebrews assumes that his readers had not yet apostatized, not that

---

[50]Kent, 113.
[51]Kent, 113.
[52]Westcott, 165.

they could not. Westcott believes apostasy is a real possibility. Guthrie understands Westcott more correctly: "The writer appears to be reflecting on a hypothetical case, although in the nature of the whole argument it must be supposed that it was a real possibility."[53]

In that sense, one may agree that the writer of Hebrews is not necessarily describing people who had already committed apostasy, as 6:9 implies. At the same time, I am confident that the passage describes apostasy as a real possibility, even if an extreme case. For the writer to describe the awful consequences that would result if people were saved and apostatized finally carries no warning value at all if it cannot happen. As Morris puts it, "Unless he is speaking of a real possibility his warning means nothing."[54] In the previous chapter I have commented on the fact that theologians who do not believe apostasy is possible do not warn believers against it!

Furthermore, the grammar of the passage is against reading it as a merely hypothetical construction. The Greeks had several ways to present hypothetical propositions: the subjunctive mode, the optative mode, even the imperfect of the indicative mode (as in 11:15, for example). But aorist participles, used as they are in this sentence, simply do not convey hypothesis. I have counted 77 other instances of the aorist participle in Hebrews, and not one of them is hypothetical—unless one counts these in 6:4-6 and those in 10:29 where the grammar and theology are the same as here.

---

[53]Guthrie, 145.
[54]Morris, 59.

If we look not at the participles but at the main clause, the writer is forthrightly saying that "It is impossible to renew [these] to repentance"—not that it would be impossible to renew them under given circumstances. The construction is exactly the same as in 6:18 (It is impossible for God to lie); 10:4 (It is impossible for the blood of bulls and goats to take away sin); and 11:6 (It is impossible to please God without faith).

In every way then the writer is saying in a straightforward manner that it is not possible to renew to repentance persons who have done the five things he lists. This warning, considered by itself or in association with the repeated warnings of the entire book, is so effective just because this apostasy is possible and recovery impossible. (Once more, I recommend the NASB translation of these verses.)

Having considered how the text is read by those who do not believe apostasy is possible, I should add for completeness that those who believe apostasy is possible but can be remedied also read the text in a way different from that which I have supported in this chapter. I have already mentioned the (somewhat different) views of Shank and Westcott to this effect and need not repeat the discussion above. I would only note that the other uses of "impossible" in Hebrews (6:18; 10:4; 11:6, as cited just above) add weight to the view that the word does not refer to a "temporary" impossibility but to something impossible by its very nature. Guthrie comments, "The statements are all absolutes."[55] McKnight, after comparing all the warning passages, concludes, "In such a context 'impossible' is to be understood as 'God

---

[55]Guthrie, 141.

will not work in them any longer so it is impossible for them to be restored'."[56]

## Conclusion

As I have noted elsewhere, one ought to derive doctrine about any subject from a passage that treats that subject directly. Hebrews 6:4-6 and the entire book seem too clear to dispute: personal apostasy from a truly regenerate condition really is possible and recovery from it impossible.

This apostasy is therefore much more serious than what most people mean by "backsliding." Since salvation is first and always by faith, this apostasy involves a willful defection from the saving knowledge of Christ, a final retraction of faith from Him in whom alone is provision for forgiveness of sins. The apostate forsakes the cross where he found redemption: "By renouncing Christ they put themselves in the position of those who, deliberately refusing His claim to be the Son of God, had Him crucified and exposed to public shame."[57]

I should probably add that such an apostate, apparently, will not desire to find forgiveness in Christ. That is precisely what he has turned away from. Those who sincerely desire forgiveness and fellowship with God have not committed apostasy. "Those who worry over whether they have committed this sin show thereby that they have not commited it.... Apostasy in Hebrews lead[s] . . . to pride in one's sinful defiance of God's will."[58]

---

[56] McKnight, 33 (note 39).

[57] Bruce, 124.

[58] McKnight, 42, 43.

I should also add that my purpose has not included developing the practical implications of this teaching. As a summary of such implications, Osborne's observations will do well: "The only remedy [against the danger of apostasy] is a constant perseverance in the faith, and a continual growth to Christian maturity."[59] Also to be noted is that the writer of Hebrews "calls his readers to assist each other by mutual exhortation on their pilgrimage journey."[60] See 3:13; 10:24f; 12:12f; 13:17.

## 2 Peter 2:18-22

For reasons of space and repetition I will not attempt so thorough a treatment of this passage as I have for Hebrews, above. Even so, it is clear to me from a careful study of the entire epistle (in even greater detail than for Hebrews) that the same kind of analysis yields the same kind of results.

Considerations of context, for example, are similarly important and indicative. The danger of apostasy is before Peter[61] throughout and is explicitly referred to in 1:8, 9 and 3:17, thus being like bookends for this brief library about the importance of spiritual growth as fortification against the apostasy of false doctrine. The passage before us provides the heart of why Peter is warning his readers so sternly.

Here is a working translation of the passage:

---

[59]Osborne, 153.

[60]Marshall, 153.

[61]I assume Simon Peter to be the inspired writer of this letter. For a defense of this view and a presentation of other introductory matters, see Robert E. Picirilli, "Commentary on the Books of 1 and 2 Peter" in *The Randall House Bible Commentary:* James, 1, 2 Peter and Jude (Nashville: Randall House Publications, 1992), 217-227.

For, uttering over-swollen (words) of empti-
ness, they [the false teachers described in the
preceding verses] lure, in lusts of the flesh with
wanton excesses, those who really (or, just
now) escaped from the ones living in error,
promising them freedom, they themselves
being slaves of corruption; for by what a person has been overcome, by this he has been
enslaved. For if, (after) escaping the pollutions
of the world by the knowledge of our Lord and
Savior Jesus Christ, they have been overcome
by being again entangled with these (pollutions), there has come to pass for them "the last
things worse than the first." For it were better
for them not to have come to the knowledge of
the way of righteousness than, (after) coming
to knowledge, to turn back from the holy commandment delivered to them. There has happened to them that of the true proverb, "A dog
returning to its vomit," and "A sow washed for a
wallowing in the mire."

A preliminary question concerns the identity of the
"they" in verse 20, who are identified as the apostates: Are
these the false teachers, or their intended victims? In
view of the fact that Peter will deal with this as an apostasy that has already occurred, I am satisfied that he is
identifying the false teachers as the apostates. However,
as Bauckham observes, "The false teachers are in the state
of definite apostasy described in verses 20-22; their followers are doubtless in severe danger of joining them."[62]

---

[62]Richard J. Bauckham, *World Biblical Commentary*: Jude, 2 Peter (Waco: Word, 1983), 277.

For our purposes here, however, it makes no difference which group Peter regards as apostates or in danger of apostasy.

The main "movements" of the passage can be indicated in a relatively simple outline:

*verses 18, 19*    the attempts of the false teachers to lure believers astray;

*verses 20, 21*    the apostasy which they exemplify;

*verse 22*    an illustrative analogy.

The key verses to consider, in discussing apostasy, therefore, are verses 20, 21. Without taking time to analyze everything leading up to them, then, I will proceed to the major questions involved.[63]

1. That these whom Peter regards as apostates had a genuine Christian experience is seen in at least three ways.

First, they "got clean away" from the pollutions of the world, which recalls 1:4. The aorist *apophugontes* (verse 20 and in 1:4) harks back to the time of their conversion.

Second, they accomplished this escape "by the knowledge of the Lord and Savior, Jesus Christ." My special study of Peter's use of *epignōsis* leaves me in no doubt that he uses this compound for knowledge consciously as a way of representing the saving knowledge of Christ one gains at conversion.[64]

Third, they "have come to know the way of righteousness." The verb "have come to know" is cognate to

---

[63] For a more thorough treatment, see Picirilli, "Commentary," 285-292.

[64] Robert E. Picirilli, "The Meaning of 'Epignōsis'" (*Evangelical Quarterly* 47:2 [1975]), 85-93.

the noun *epign-osis* just referred to, and is used with the same meaning. That it is perfect tense focuses on the state of knowledge that followed the initiation therein. The "way of righteousness" is obviously the same as "the way of truth" in verse 2 and "the straight way" in verse 15.

As I have observed, above, in reference to the four expressions used in Hebrews 6:4-6, it would be hard to find a better description of what it means to become a Christian. Bauckham, after comparing the words here with those used in 1:3, 4, concludes that they are similar because "this is the vocabulary in which our author expresses the essential content of Christianity."[65]

2. The apostasy which Peter ascribes to these and warns his readers against is found in two expressions, each standing in sharp contrast to the experience just described.

First, they "have been overcome by being again entangled with these (pollutions)." And this after their escape from those very pollutions! In light of verse 19b, this being overcome is being re-enslaved. Clearly, these apostates have returned to the practice of the fleshly wickedness that previously defiled them.

Nor does the fact that this is introduced with an "if" mitigate this conclusion. This is a first class condition in Greek, the "if" of reality which might as well be translated "since." Even Kistemaker, a thorough-going Calvinist, acknowledges that the ones referred to were once "orthodox Christians" who "escaped the world's defilements"—and then hurries to make these "orthodox Christians" orthodox in external profession and lifestyle only.[66] He apparently does not realize how self-contra-

---

[65]Bauckham, 276.

dictory this sounds, or how unlike Peter's more obvious meaning.

Second, they have come to the place where they "turn back from the holy commandment delivered to them." And this after having come to know the way of righteousness! The "holy commandment" may be "the moral law of the gospel,"[67] or the whole range of gospel truth,[68] or better "Christianity as a whole way of life."[69] It was "delivered to them" when the gospel was preached to them and its implications taught. It is a holy commandment because it sets people apart as God's and teaches them a way of life appropriate for saints.

3. The seriousness of this apostasy Peter indicates in two expressions and a proverb.

First, "the last things have come to be worse for them than the first." No doubt Peter is alluding to Jesus' words in Matthew 12:45 and sees that principle fulfilled in the experience of these apostates. They are in worse condition than before they came to the saving knowledge described above.

Second, "it were better for them not to have come to know the way of righteousness." This is an incredibly startling thing: can anything be worse than never having come to the saving knowledge of the way of the Lord? As Kelly notes, apostates are worse off than unconvert-

---

[66]Simon J. Kistemaker, *New Testament Commentary: Peter and Jude* (Grand Rapids: Baker, 1987), 311, 312.

[67]Henry Alford, *The Greek Testament,* vol. 4 (Cambridge: Deighton, Bell and Co., 1871), 411.

[68]R. C. H. Lenski, *The Interpretation of the Epistles of St. Peter, St. John, and St. Jude* (Columbus, Ohio: Brethren Book Concern, 1938), 340.

[69]J. N. D. Kelly, *A Commentary on the Epistles of Peter and Jude* (Grand Rapids: Baker, 1981 reprint), 350.

ed unbelievers "because they have rejected the light."[70] And if our study, above, of Hebrews has led us to the right conclusions, we understand even better why Peter puts this so strongly. An apostate cannot be recovered; a never converted unbeliever can.

Third, Peter illustrates with a two-fold proverbial saying (or with two proverbial sayings). That the idea proverbially represented "has happened" to the apostates means that the proverbs fit their situation. Like a dog that comes back to lick up the spoiled vomit that sickened him in the first place, like a sow that gets a bath and goes back to the mud from which she had been cleansed, these apostates return to the enslaving, polluting wickedness from which they had been delivered.

Those who attempt to mitigate Peter's teaching by suggesting that the real nature of the sow or the dog had not been changed, and that this implies that these apostate false teachers were never regenerated, are pressing the illustrations beyond what they are intended to convey. Indeed, the proverbs must be interpreted by the clearer words that precede them and not the other way around. The previous paragraph expresses precisely what the proverbs are intended to convey.

In conclusion, it is clear that Peter is describing a real apostasy from genuine Christianity. I will not pursue the passage further and respond to Calvinistic interpretations since this would be essentially repetition of my response to the Calvinistic interpretations of Hebrews, above.

---

[70]Kelly, 349.

## For Further Reading About the Biblical Teaching on Apostasy

Marshall, I. H. *Kept By the Power of God*. Minneapolis: Bethany Fellowship, 1969.

McKnight, Scot. "The Warning Passages of Hebrews: A Formal Analysis and Theological Conclusions," in *Trinity Journal* 13NS (1992), 21-59.

Osborne, Grant R. "Soteriology in the Epistle to the Hebrews," in *Grace Unlimited*, ed. Clark Pinnock. Grand Rapids: Bethany Fellowship, 1975, 144-166.

Shank, Robert. *Life in the Son*. Springfield, Mo.: Westcott Publishers, 1960. [Shank's views are not entirely parallel to those of this writer.]

## Grace, Faith, Free Will
**Robert E. Picirilli**

Though he presents both classic Calvinism and Arminianism in order to help readers intelligently decide for themselves, Dr. Picirilli unashamedly advocates a very specific form of Arminianism as the best resolution of the tensions between the two doctrinal positions. In what he calls "Reformation Arminianism," Picirilli reclaims the original views of Arminius and his defenders.

ISBN 0892656484 - $19.99

## The Quest For Truth: Answering Life's Inescapable Questions
**F. Leroy Forlines**

This invaluable tool discusses profound truths that apply to every facet of life. Forlines asserts that biblical truth should be make applicable to the total personality. These "inescapable questions of life" are answered from the standard of God's authoritative Word.

ISBN 0892659629 paperback - $29.99
ISBN 0892658649 hardback  - $34.99

## Randall House Ministers Manual & New Testament

The *Randall House Ministers Manual* is an essential resource for any minister. The manual includes the entire New Testament and Psalms text as well as sample wedding services, funeral services, baby dedications, and much more.

ISBN 0892655402 - $17.99

## Regaining Balance: 91 Days of Prayer and Praise
**Randy Sawyer**

*Regaining Balance* is a devotional journal designed to guide its readers through a season of spiritual revival. A free, on-line Leader's Guide (www.RandallHouse.com) allows pastors and Bible study leaders to utilize this devotional in a group setting.

ISBN 0892655186 - $9.99
Bulk discounts available

To order visit *www.RandallHouse.com* or call 1-800-877-7030.

Printed in the United States
55803LVS00001B/271-324